Prov
Sayings of an Ordinary Man

WHAT IS A POET?

A poet is one licensed to carry live words, living words
His words, however, should always remain holstered
unless in meter or verse
Not necessarily in rhyme for rhyme has served its time.

Why is the poet granted this license?
It is because language is often very sedate
needing someone to put life into it
To make ordinary speech worth listening to.

How does the poet do this?
On the license it states that he should be one gifted in the perception and expression of the beautiful or lyrical or that he should have crafted the art of bringing life to language.

It further states that he should have mastered comparisons, handling with ease — similes, metaphors, and personifications. That he uses them with caution and not with reckless abandon. The license also numerates other figures of the comparative type that the poet should have in his arsenal, namely: synesthesia, synecdoche, epithets, metonymies, and oxymora.

Anyone well qualified in the aforementioned areas should have no trouble in being granted a poet's license.

Luther Whitley

Proverbial Sayings of an Ordinary Man

and selected poems

Luther Whitley

Introduction by
V. Lois Taylor

VERACITY PUBLISHING
WASHINGTON, DC

Copyright © LD Whitley 2006

Published by Veracity Publishing
P.O. Box 70087
Washington, D.C. 20024
202-236-1541 FAX 202-544-4482
ldcoolwhit@aol

All rights reserved. Except for the quotation of short passages for the purposes of criticism and review, no part of this publication may be reproduced, stored in a retrieval system, or transmitted, in any form or by any means, electronic, mechanical, photocopying, recording or otherwise, without the permission of the publisher.

Unless otherwise noted, all Bible quotations and citations are from the Holy Bible, New International Version, ® Copyright © 1973,1978,1984, International Bible Society. Used by permission.

PRINTED IN THE UNITED STATES OF AMERICA
ISBN 0-975 5469-2-9

CONTENTS

CONTENTS...v
ACKNOWLEDGMENTS..x
INTRODUCTION.. xii

Chapter 1 COMBINING SPIRITUAL MATTERS WITH SPIRITUAL WORDS 1

Hebrew Poetry... 2
God Wants To Be Famous...4
Listen To The Wise Man..5
About God..6
Jesus Knew His Bible (What About You?)....................7
Fame And Glory...9
The Positive Power Of Prayer..................................10
Jesus Christ Is..11
Man Was Created To Live Forever............................12
Biblical Movies..13
Get To Know God...14
Jesus Wants You..16
Where Do We Belong?...18
The Only Reason To Boast......................................20
Do You Know Me?..22
How We Show Our Love..23
Faith Is...24
Not Of The Twelve 25
Say The Name..26
Death Is 27
In God's Image...28
Uninvited..29
The Height Of Stupidity..30
The Garden of Eden...32

One God, One Name..34
You Say Shăd, I Say Shā..35
Armageddon Is..36
The Truth Will Set You Free..37
Hell Is..40
Have You Ever Wondered Why?..41
True Happiness..43
Love Is...44

Chapter 2 AND THEN THERE IS LOVE................ 45
Distant Lovers...46
And Then There Is Love...47
June (A Song)...48
Falling In Love...49
Something Beautiful..52
They're Not The Same..54

Chapter 3 THE MATING GAME..............................56
How They Find a Mate...57
Butting Heads...58
The Plight Of An Arachnid..59
A Ball Of Fun...60
Why Does the Firefly Flash?...61
He Understands Pregnancy..62

Chapter 4 THE DATING GAME..............................63
No Dating..64
If It Suits Them, Fine...65
Why I Can Never Be, "Just Friends"...................................66

Chapter 5 CAPITAL PUNISHMENT......67
Not Playing God..68
Does God Get Upset?.......................................69
Where Murderers Belong..................................70
Does The State Have The Right?.....................71
Murderers: Useless People...............................72
When Should Murders Be Forgiven?...............73
A Time To Be Leery...74
A Big Difference...75
"Thou Shall Not Kill".......................................77
The Guilty Party...78

Chapter 6 ABOUT CARS.........................79
Miss Ann...80
Buddy...81
Mr. Walker's International...............................83

Chapter 7 ABOUT PEOPLE....................84
Lazy People Are Crazy People.........................85
Who's Your Daddy?...86
Katrina, Katrina..87
Mother's, No..89
Subterranean Man...90
Mother's Prized Possession..............................91
Spoiled Soda?...93
Um Um Good...94
Good Pancakes...95
Something Nice..96
My Favorite Drink..98
That Woman (A Song).....................................99
Sleeping Beauty..101

To Be A Poet..102

Chapter 8 PHILOSOPHY......................................103
The Hypocrisy Of Democracy.........................104
Stop The Bitchin'...107
Cancel That Subscription..................................114
The Vanity Of Profanity....................................115
The Greatest Nation..117
Expansion..118
A Little More Of The Beautiful, Please...........119

Chapter 9 A GUY THING..120
With What Do You Think?...............................121
My Favorite Things...122
No Brainer...123
My Ultimate High...124
I Know Where I Am...125

Chapter 10 ABOUT GUNS......................................126
In Guns We Trust..127
Americans Love Guns......................................128
Quick Draw..129

Chapter 11 PROVERBIAL SAYINGS....................130
God..132
The Bible...133
Knowledge And Wisdom..................................134
God's Ministers...136
Church Ministers..137
Foolish Ones...138
Death...139

Worldly Persons..140
Integrity...141

Chapter 12 HAIKU: BRIEF AND TO THE POINT..142
Haiku# 1 Summer..143
Haiku# 2 Fall...143
Haiku# 3 Winter..143
Haiku# 4 Spring..143
Haiku# 5 The Rainbow...143
Haiku # 6 Why The Rainbow?..................................143
Haiku # 7 Day Or Night..143
Haiku # 8 A Blanket...143
Haiku # 9 What Time Is It?......................................143
Haiku #10 The Black Widow Male..........................143

ACKNOWLEDGMENTS

The majority of my poems and proverbial sayings are based on the Scriptures and so I thank Almighty God first and foremost for giving us his Word. I thank him for giving me the ability to understand, comprehend and appreciate his Word. I thank him for such men as Solomon who wrote many of the Proverbs and David, his father, who wrote many of the Psalms which contains some of the most beautiful poetry but much more.

Thanks to my son, Luther and daughters, Denise and Joanne not only for their support but also for being the subject or narrator of at least four of my poems.

I thank my assistant, Minnie L. Cooper, for her hard work, helping me with research and typing, as well as, all of the other little things, it took to complete this book.

Special thanks to Gloria Butler who I could call at anytime to use as a sounding board. I thank her for always listening and for all of her fine suggestions.

A thank you to my long time friend Geraldine Williams for her help in typing and for the tools she supplied that were so beneficial to the completion of this book.

Thank you to my dear friend Lillie Taylor who is always my first reviewer.

A very special thank you to my long time friend Cheryl Allen for her support, for all of the tips, advice and suggestions she gave me for this project.

Thanks to long time friends and supporters, Elease Hall, Regina Rogers, Kita Adams, Ambassador Ronald Palmer, Bernie Walker, Julia Scott, Sandy Lucas, Naomi

Mitchell, Al and Gita Morris, Betty Land, Dr. Pearl Wisham Perry, Kimberlin Love, Mahboob Ahmed, Charles and Delores Huddleston, Wylie and June Selden, Denise Washington, William and Eugenia Dixon, Misty Robinson, Leonard Grant, Mary Fields, Larnita Plummer, Yvonne Young, LaVerne Gaynor, Dr. Clifford Lee, Patricia Gies, and Kimberly C. Turner.

I am especially grateful to J. Joy Matthews Alford, a.k.a., Sistah Joy, a wonderful poet and host of Verse, Vibes and Bites where this book is scheduled to be released.

Last, but by no means least, I thank Dr. V. Lois Taylor, Professor, Howard University English Department who I feel a deep debt of gratitude for accepting and introducing my first book of poetry and wise sayings with words not only gracious but with words that capture the very essence of my poems and sayings.

INTRODUCTION

To introduce Luther Whitley's newest book, ***Proverbial Sayings of an Ordinary Man***, is a true delight! The book, aptly titled, is comprised of poetry and prose — reflective of the voice of one who refers to himself as an "ordinary man." This collection of *literary gems* should captivate an audience with inspiration and entertainment.

Clearly, Whitley's books define him as a man who possesses in depth knowledge and understanding of the Holy Bible. Without reservation, he demonstrates the ability to convey the divine message through the use of his unique rhetorical strategies. Furthermore, ***Proverbial Sayings of an Ordinary Man*** holds for its readers an appeal that is lighthearted and enchanting.

In the first chapter, *Combining Spiritual Matters with Spiritual Words,* his poems, in a manner that is similar to the Psalms, magnify and glorify the Creator. Just as the Psalmists achieve this type of mastery, Whitley accomplishes his rhetorical task with the power and beauty of poetic parallelism and contrast that are so characteristic of Hebrew verse. Hence, the poems in this chapter convey the Creator's primary purpose of having all earthy creatures exalt his name.

Whitley's love poems in Chapter 2, *And Then There is Love* contain two masterpieces: "Falling in Love," and "They're Not the Same." Poems in the remaining chapters relate to almost every facet of life. They range from the humorous to the solemn. "Butting Heads," Chapter 3, "Lazy People are Crazy People" and "Sleeping Beauty" of Chapter 7, and "I Know Where I Am," Chapter 9 are good examples of the writer's humor. On a more serious note, are the following: "When Should Murderers be Forgiven?", Chapter 5, "The Hypocrisy of Democracy," Chapter 8, and "In Guns We Trust," Chapter 10.

While most of his proverbial sayings are expressed in pithy sentences, they make a strong impact and are thought provoking. In retrospect, Chapter 1, offers the readers something to which they can look forward: "Where Do We Belong?", "Man Was Created to Live Forever" and "The Garden of Eden."

UNDENIABLY, LUTHER WHITLEY IS A WRITER WHOSE INSIGHT AND CREATIVITY REMAIN UNPARALLELED. His name is sure to resurface on the literary scene in the future!

V. Lois Taylor
April 2006

Chapter 1 COMBINING SPIRITUAL MATTERS WITH SPIRITUAL WORDS

Humans exist on this planet for but one primary reason and that reason is to praise, honor, and to give glory to God. Certainly if the material universe gives glory to God how much more so should humans.

In all that we do and in all that we say we should have in mind giving glory to God.

This is what the spiritual person does for he is always combining spiritual matters with spiritual words.

HEBREW POETRY

Since many of my poems are based on the Scriptures especially the Psalms and Proverbs, the two most poetic books, I decided to write some of them in the Hebrew style of poetry. Hebrew poetic lines are short — many are no more than two or three words — making the total effect one of strong impact.

The most important formal element in Hebrew poetry is parallelism, or rhythm achieved, not by rhyme (as in English), but by logical thought; it has been called "sense rhythm." Notice the first two lines of **GOD WANTS TO BE FAMOUS**, page 4:

God wants to be famous,
Fame and glory He wants for himself

The lines quoted above are said to be in *synonymous parallelism*, that is, the second line repeats a portion of the previous line, but in different words. The phrase "wants to be famous" is actually found in both lines, in the second line the words are inverted and slightly different but say essentially the same thing.

There are at least two other primary styles of parallelism:

In *antithetic parallelism*, as the designation implies each line expresses contrary thoughts. **LISTEN TO THE WISE MAN**, page 5 illustrates this:

The senseless one says, there is no God, that we evolved from lower primates.
Moses, a wise man said, "The Lord God formed the man from

the dust of the ground."

Then there is *synthetic* (or formal, constructive) *parallelism* in which the second portion does not simply echo the same thought as the first or give a contrast. Rather, it enlarges and adds a new thought. **ABOUT GOD**, page 6 is an example of this:

> *The name of God is a strong tower,*
> *a source of refuge for the righteous ones.*
> *The word of God is alive and exerts power.*
> *Is sharper than any two-edged sword.*
> *The spirit of God searches into all things*
> *even the deep things of God.*

Notice that the second part of each sentence or clause completes the thought; the whole verse, therefore is a synthesis, that is, the result of bringing together two elements. Only with the second half-lines, such as "a source of refuge for the righteous ones" and "is sharper than any two-edged sword" does the reader learn how "the name of God is a strong tower" and how "the word of God is alive and exerts power." In such a series of synthetic parallels, this division between the first and second part serves as a rhythmic break. There is thus, along with the progression of thought, the preservation of a certain verse structure, a parallel of form. It is for this reason sometimes called formal or *constructive parallelism.*

GOD WANTS TO BE FAMOUS

God wants to be famous
    Fame and glory he wants for himself
God wants his name praised, honored and respected
    He wants his name to be glorified
Humans don't want God to be famous
    They don't want God's name known above all others
Humans seek fame and glory for themselves
    They want their own names to be famous
Some say that for God to have a name belittles him
    They say that God is too great to have a name
One name for God is not enough others say
    They say that God has many names
God gave himself his one personal name
    His is a self-given personal name
Bible translators don't like God's name
    They prefer the titles Adhonay and Elohim to God's name
They rendered the tetragrammaton which stands for
    God's personal name as either Lord or God
All haters of God's name will suffer, for Asaph makes
    This request of God:
"Fill their faces with shame; that they may seek thy
    Name, O Lord
Let them be confounded and troubled forever; yea,
    Let them be put to shame, and perish
That men may know that thou, whose name alone
    Is JE - HŌ ' VAH, art the most high over all the earth"

                                Ps. 83:18 KJV, 1611

LISTEN TO THE WISE MAN

    The senseless one says there is no God
    That we evolved from lower primates
Moses, a wise man said: "God formed the man from dust of the ground"
    The senseless one says that the universe is the result of some cosmological big bang
Paul said: "Every house is constructed by someone but he who constructed all things is God."
    The senseless one says that humans are capable in themselves of guiding their own destiny
Jeremiah said: "It does not belong to man who is walking even to direct his step."
    The senseless one says that the Bible is man's word and that it is faulty
Peter said: "No prophecy of scripture springs from any private interpretation. For prophecy was at no time brought by man's will, but men spoke from God as they were borne along by Holy Spirit."
    The senseless one says that the earth and its inhabitants will suffer a cosmological or nuclear annihilation.
David said: "The righteous themselves will possess the earth, and they will reside forever upon it."

ABOUT GOD

The Name of God is a strong tower
    A source of refuge for the righteous ones
The Word of God is alive and exerts power
    Is sharper than any two-edged sword
The Spirit of God searches into all things
    Even the deep things of God
The Love of God is everlasting
    Nothing can separate us from God's love
The Righteousness of God is enduring
    Righteous and upright is he, always
The Day of God is coming, a fear-inspiring day
    Seek God now and you may be concealed in
    The day of his anger.

JESUS KNEW HIS BIBLE (What About You?)

He entered the synagogue
    This was his custom on the Sabbath Day
From the scroll of Isaiah he found
    Where it was written about him
Scriptures in those days were not divided
into chapters and verses
    He read the Scripture he wanted
Applied it properly and then sat down
    Jesus knew his Bible, what about you?

Hungry after fasting for forty days
    He was challenged by the Devil to prove
himself a Son of God by turning stones into loaves
    He responded: "It is written, 'Man must live not on bread alone but on every word that comes from the mouth of God.' "
    Jesus knew his Bible, what about you?

Challenged to jump off a cliff to see if God would save him
    He responded: "It is written, 'Do not put the Lord your God to the test.' "
    Jesus knew his Bible, what about you?

Offered world rulership by the Devil if he would bow down
    in worship to him
Jesus responded: "It is written, 'Worship the Lord your God and serve him only.' "
    Jesus knew his Bible, what about you?

Tested with a trick question on the resurrection Jesus responded: "It is written, 'In the resurrection neither do men marry nor are women given in marriage.' "
Jesus knew his Bible, what about you?

Are you a follower of Jesus?
When your faith is questioned can you like him say: "It is written?"

FAME AND GLORY

For himself he wants fame and glory
    He wants it to be that everybody knows his name
He wants his name to stand out
    To rise above all others
He wants no one to question who he is
    He wants all to know who he is
When names are brought up
    He wants his name right up there
When name dropping is done
    He wants his to be the one
He wants his enemies to shudder
    At the very sound of his name
He wants his name to invoke awe and respect
    Yes, for himself he wants fame and glory
And what's wrong with wanting fame and glory
    For yourself when you deserve it?
When you're GOD

THE POSITIVE POWER OF PRAYER

Prayer is worshipful address to God
    Causally talking to God is not prayer
Prayer is not just from the lips but from the heart
    Simply repeating someone else's words is not prayer
Prayer should express your own sentiments
    Reciting something by rote is not prayer
Prayer need not always be audible
    Being from the heart prayer can be silent
Prayer can never successfully be restricted,
    Banished or outlawed from anywhere
For as long as you have a heart and are conscious you can pray
Prayer involves devotion, trust, respect and a sense of
    dependence on the one prayed to.
Belief in God and knowledge of his will is
    essential to having one's prayers answered
How positively powerful is prayer?
    You can be locked up in an iron-clad cell
    but your prayers will go right through that iron
How positively penetrating is prayer?
    You can be held captive in the ground in a concrete
    bunker but your prayer will go straight through that
    concrete
How depth defying is prayer?
    You can be 20,000 leagues under the sea but your
    prayer will go right up from the ocean floor, right up
    to God in heaven without anything or anyone being
    able to hinder it, slow it down or stop it.
For that is the positive power of prayer.

JESUS CHRIST IS

Jesus Christ is not an idol
    He is our exemplar, our model
Jesus Christ is not God incarnate
    He is the Son of God
Jesus Christ is God's Only-Begotten Son
    As the Word he was God's only direct creation
God used the Word in the creation of all other things
    By means of him all other things were created in the
Heavens and upon the earth
Jesus Christ is wisdom personified
    He has the power of God and the wisdom of God
Jesus Christ is the Word of God, God's Chief spokesman
    He said: "What I teach is not mine, but belongs to
    Him that sent me
Jesus Christ is our Prince of Life
    There is no salvation in anyone else, for there is not
another name under heaven that has been given among men
by which we must get saved
Jesus Christ is a mighty God, but not almighty
    He said: "The Father is greater than I am."

MAN WAS CREATED TO LIVE FOREVER

How do we know that man was
    created to live forever?
This we can figure out by being
    just a little clever
There was only one reason why man
    would ever die
Eating from the forbidden fruit was
    the only reason why
Had they never eaten from that
    forbidden tree
They would have never died but
    kept on living, eternally
Since God never wanted them
    to disobey
He likewise never wanted them
    to pass away
It was only after they ate
    the forbidden fruit
That from the garden did they
    get the boot
To keep them from getting back in
    and eating from the tree of life
God posted angels at the entrance
    guarding it both day and night
While man is born to die
He was not created to die
That is why Jesus came to earth to die
So man would no longer have to die.

BIBLICAL MOVIES

Who needs a movie
    To bolster their faith?
Not real Christians,
    Just those who perpetrate
Biblical movies by worldlings
    are bound to be flawed
Therefore, real Christians
    are not by them awed
Real Christians know the truth
    They've got it right
They therefore walk by faith
    and not by sight

GET TO KNOW GOD

The most important thing
    that can ever be done
Is to get to know the true God
    and his Son
To merely say that you are a believer
    just won't do
For did you not know
    that the Devil is a believer too!
A good working knowledge of God's Word
    is just the place to start
But you must come to love God
    with your whole soul, mind, and heart
His loving kindness and mercy
    we must learn to appreciate
But his divine justice and retribution
    we must never ever under estimate
Getting to know God
    means more than just going to church
It means opening up his Word and
    making a thorough search
Getting to know God
    means following closely his son
Thinking and acting like Jesus
    with him becoming as one.
Getting to know God makes
    everything clear
Lets us know where we came from and
    why we are here.

Getting to know God leads to
    a happy life
Gives us true peace of mind and joy
    amid this world and all of its strife.
Getting to know God, it is him
    that we imitate
We therefore practice showing love
    and not hate.
Getting to know God, always
    having him in mind
We therefore become patient,
    long-suffering and kind.
Encouraging and up building is
    how we are always found
The kind of people that others
    always love to be around.
By getting to know God and
    accepting Jesus' sacrifice
We get all of these things now
    as well as life eternal in paradise.

JESUS WANTS YOU

Are you conscious of your spiritual need?
Are you in need of a spiritual awakening?
Are you depressed, burdened or weighted down?
Are you lost but with a burning desire to be found?

Then Jesus wants you

Are you a fine physical specimen
    But aching for something you're not sure of?
Are you weak, frail or sickly
    But your spirit is willing?
Are you intelligent, bright and witty
    But love the taste of humble pie?
Are you slow, not so smart
    But full of goodness from your heart?

Then Jesus wants you

Do you have great material wealth
    But happiness still eludes you?
Are you poor, lacking in the necessities of life
    But long most of all to be spiritually rich?
Are you crooked and immoral
    But really want to change?
Are you kind, mild and meek
    And is getting to know Jesus what you really seek?

Then Jesus wants you

Do you go the church for all
      the wrong reasons?
Do you go only on certain days
      and only in certain seasons?
Are you without care, worry or concern
      If that's the case, you've got a lot to learn?

Jesus may still want you

"Come to me," He says, "All you who are weary and burdened . . . . learn from me . . . . and you will find rest . . . . for my yoke is easy and my burden is light.

WHERE DO WE BELONG?

There is a reason why
We love a beautiful garden or park
Why we love walking through the woods
Anytime before it gets dark

There is a reason why
We love pretty flowers, leaves and trees
Why we love playing in the sand and
Watching and listening to the birds and bees

There is a reason why
We love shedding our clothes
On those mild sun shiny days
Why we love frolicking in the water
Or just relaxing, soaking up some rays

There is a reason why
Luscious ripe fruit is such a lovely sight
Why about the only thing better
Is the taking of a bite.

There is a reason why
Our comfortable homes we sometimes leave
To pitch a tent outside
Kind of hard for some to conceive

There is a reason why
Some find critters such a delight
Why some take to animals
Without a hint of fright.

There is a reason why
We love a beautiful garden or park
It is because a beautiful garden was our home
We were created to live in Paradise
We were made from the earth
To live in Paradise on the earth

Earth is our home
Somewhere it even says:
"The meek will inherit the earth
And live forever upon it"
Yes, we belong in Paradise
A beautiful garden or park
Paradise is our home
Paradise is our destiny.

THE ONLY REASON TO BOAST

There are things we think too little of
There are things we think too much of
Things thought too much of,
Nation . . . . Race . . . . Gender

FOR WHAT IS A NATION?
But a location, a country where you live
Either by choice, but in most cases, by chance

AND WHAT IS RACE?
But the genus or group into which
You were . . . . Born

AND WHAT IS GENDER?
But a few chromosomes
You have of your own

So let no one brag about his
Country . . . . you didn't establish the country
Neither should one boast about
The skin he's in . . . . you didn't create the races
Nor should one proclaim any splendor of
His gender . . . . you didn't create the sexes

Just like everyone else, you have these things
Because you received them
So let no one boast about any of these things
But if one must boast
Let him boast of something really important

Let him boast of this very thing,
The having of insight and the having
of knowledge of the True and Almighty God

THE ONLY REASON TO BOAST

DO YOU KNOW ME?

Many are the Ones who keep **Looking** for Me
    From time Indefinite to time Indefinite
Many are the Ones who keep **Calling Out** for Me
    From Generation to Generation
Many have **Voiced** a burning desire for Me
    During all of their Waking Hours
Many are the Ones who keep **Diligently Seeking** Me
    Even in their Nocturnal Images
As for hidden treasure many keep **Searching** for Me
    On Land and Sea and in the Skies
Many are the Ones always in **Constant Pursuit** of Me
    From Sunrise to Sunset
Few have **Actually Found** Me
    But then, Discovered They couldn't Handle Me
Who Am I? What Am I?

One thing to you but another to another
This is something that I am not

Universal I Am, The Same The Whole World Over
I Certify, I Verify, I Rectify!

Do You Know Me?

I Am The Truth!

HOW WE SHOW OUR LOVE

Nothing better can one be doing
Than to spend one's life pursuing,
    Pursuing knowledge of the One
    Who gave His only begotten Son
Gave him to straighten out our undoing
Tho' we did not deserve this love
It stopped Him not from showing His love
    So how do we demonstrate
    That His love we appreciate?
Obeying His commands is how we show our love

FAITH IS

Faith is being sure of what we hope for
      and certain of what we do not see
How can we be so sure of what we hope for?
      This assurance results from knowledge
Thus faith is based on knowledge
      The more knowledge one has
The more faith one can have

Little or no knowledge, little or no faith.

NOT OF THE TWELVE

He was not of the twelve
Not a replacement for any of the twelve
But he outshone many of the twelve
He traveled more than many of the twelve
Wrote more than any of the twelve
Where does he stand in relation to the twelve?
He really should not be compared to the twelve
His assignment was different than the twelve
So he is not included in John's vision of the twelve
Paul was apostle to the nations and so not of the twelve

SAY THE NAME

When before Pharaoh, Moses didn't say, "the Lord,
the God of Israel says: Let my people go"
Moses used the divine name, Jehovah
Saying the "Lord sent me" would have meant nothing to
Pharaoh, a man of many gods

David didn't say, "The Lord is my shepherd."
David used God's personal name, Jehovah
Having a close personal relationship with God, David most
often addressed God by his personal name

Isaiah didn't say, "The Lord is my strength"
He used God's personal name, Jehovah

How do we know this? Because in all of these instances,
"Lord" is rendered from the Tetragrammaton.

What is the Tetragrammaton? It is the four Hebrew letters
יהוה usually transliterated as YHWH or JHVH (Yahweh or
Jehovah) representing God's memorial name.

DEATH IS

Live your life as one with hope in the resurrection
As one who knows what death really is
As one who knows the true condition of the dead
That when you die you have nothing at all
That there is no knowledge, no wisdom, no conscious
Thought, no feelings in death
That torture and torment are not possible after death
Death is not a change in life nor a transferral of life
But the complete end of life
Death is an unconscious condition
Like sleep but without dreams
The dead are awakened only through the resurrection
The dead are alive only in someone else's memory,
Hopefully in God's memory

IN GOD'S IMAGE

Created in God's image,
    what does that mean?
Not that we look like God
    for God is a spirit
It means that humans have
    certain qualities like God
Certain qualities that animals
    don't have
Only humans have true wisdom
    which starts with knowing God
Only humans have true love
    based on an unselfish interest in another
Only humans manifest true justice
    the ability to calculate fairness and impartiality
Only humans have true power
    the ability to harness the elements for man's good
Never, ever, will you hear an animal say
    about any of these things: "Oh, I can do that!"

UNINVITED

When he comes to visit
    He has usually been uninvited
Thoughtless and inconsiderate
    He has always been
Tho' he often comes to visit, he is
    anything but a friend
For he never comes to visit
    lest he takes someone away
Bringing grief and sorrow to all
    of those who then must stay
But there is good news,
    his days are numbered
The day is coming when he
    must return those he has taken
After which he will be consigned
    to the lake that burns with fire and sulfur
Then the saying will take place that is written:
    "Death, where is your victory?"
    "Death, where is your sting?"

THE HEIGHT OF STUPIDITY

Tall and upright it stood
In all of its majesty
But down to earth it came
Felled by his ax and his savagery

Into lengths it was cut
To fit the fireplace
To heat that big open room
To heat that big black cooking pot

Picking up an idle log
He began to carve
And slowly it began to take shape
After some time it now had a face

It was not that of his father
It was not the face of his mother
Neither was it his sister nor brother
It was the face .... of his god

He continued his carving
And a mouth it had, but it could not speak
Eyes it had, but it could not see
Ears it had, but it could not hear
A nose it had, but it could not smell

Yes, into a god itself, into a carved image
he cut the log
He then prostrates himself to it and
bows down and prays to it

And he also says to it: "Deliver me, for you are my god"
The truth is that in the case of danger, in the case of a fire
that he would have to deliver his god, showing that
fashioning, building, constructing one's own god is the
height of stupidity.

THE GARDEN OF EDEN

Beautiful it was, very beautiful
    Like a lady whose every feature was perfect
Perfect hair, perfect eyes, perfect nose, perfect mouth,
    perfect body
That is how Eden was, beautiful
    The garden of God, man's original home
It had been specially made by the Great Landscaper
    Specially made for man to cultivate and take care of
As his family grew, man would grow the garden
    Grow it til the entire earth was like Eden
Til the earth was filled with never dying perfect people
In Eden a river ran through it
    A river to water the garden
And God made to grow out of the ground
    Every tree desirable to one's sight and good for food
The most beautiful forest, the most beautiful garden,
    The most beautiful park that you have ever seen
All of these pale in comparison to the beautiful
    Garden of Eden
Have you ever seen grass so lush and green
    So beautiful that you dare not walk on it
Well, Eden would have made it look like a cow pasture
Have you ever seen trees so magnificent
    that they looked like the work of an artist brush
The trees of Eden would have made them
    look like the disenchanted forest
Have you ever seen fruit so beautiful and so luscious
    that you didn't want to mar it with a bite

Well, the fruit of the trees of Eden
    would have made that fruit animal feed
Adam and Eve were evicted from their beautiful garden home
    Evicted for failure to pay the mortgage
And what was the mortgage requirement?
    Not eating from one certain tree
Disobedience caused man to lose his beautiful Paradise Home
    But this did not thwart God's purpose
So, in due time this earth will become a Paradise, a Beautiful Garden, a Beautiful Park

For God's purpose can never fail.

ONE GOD, ONE NAME

God is not a name
    But a title
Lord is not a name
    But a title
Father is not a name
    But a title
Almighty is not a name
    But a title
Adonay is Hebrew for Lord
    Therefore not a name
Elohim' is Hebrew for God
    Therefore not a name
God gave himself only one
    Personal name, Jehovah
At times God wanted his name
    Remembered in a special way
And so at times he enlarged
    His name making it:
Jehovah Himself is There
Jehovah is our Righteousness
Jehovah - Jireh
Jehovah - Nissi
Jevovah of Armies
These expressions only amplify
God's One Name, Jehovah

YOU SAY SHĂD, I SAY SHĀ

The dictionary
pronounces it as Shăd´răk
The Bible, Shā´drăk

ARMAGEDDON IS

Armageddon is,
When correctly understood
More than just the final war,
The evil versus the good

Armageddon is,
According to the Revelation
God's war in which he fights against
All the earthly nations

World leaders and their armies
Unite in this fight against God
They are emboldened to fight this war
Because of having Satan's prod.

All of man's governments at
Armageddon will fall
Democratic, Communistic, Totalitarian;
God will eliminate them all

Jesus Christ, who will be
Leader of God's forces
Annihilates the nations armies
Trampling them as if astride gigantic horses

Armageddon is God's war
A great and fear-inspiring day
Leaving only those on earth
Who love doing things His way.

THE TRUTH WILL SET YOU FREE

Knowing God's Truth is what sets one free.
Do you know God's Truth?
If the cares and worries of day to day
living overwhelm you
Then God's Truth you need to know

If what politicians do or say unduly concern you
Then God's Truth you need to know

If you are preoccupied with
the problems of race, nation or gender
Then God's Truth you need to know

If you are constantly complaining
about your lot in life, jealous of
what others may have achieved
Then God's Truth you need to know

If you are still asking where we
came and why are we here
Then God's Truth you need to know

If you think that acquiring material wealth
will make you truly happy
Then God's Truth you need to know

If you think that killing your fellow man is okay
as long as its in war
Then God's Truth you need to know

If you think that being a church
minister automatically makes one
a minister of God
Then God's Truth you need to know

If you think that by merely going to
church you'll get saved
Then God's Truth you need to know

If you think that the use of idols and images
are acceptable in worship to God
Then God's Truth you need to know

If you think that some man has taken
Jesus' place on earth or that a man
can forgive sins
Then God's Truth you need to know

If you do not have true peace of mind, contentment
and joy, even in this strife-torn world
Then God's Truth you need to know

If you are not thoroughly familiar with
the Bible, acknowledging that "All Scripture
is inspired of God and beneficial for
teaching, for reproving and setting things straight."
Then God's Truth you need to know

If you think that the dead are somehow
still alive or that God tortures or
torments people
Then God's Truth you need to know

If you are not laughed at for being
different, ridiculed and persecuted
for your faith
Then you do not know God's Truth

And if you do not know the Truth..........
you are not free, but in slavery.

HELL IS

Hell is mankind's common grave
It is the abode of the dead
Not a place of punishment
But a place of rest and hope instead

Tormented, Job prayed to go to hell
He wanted to die and go to the grave
There to stay until the resurrection
From his persecutors having been saved

Jesus went to hell
Not because he stole, cheated or lied
For Jesus was perfect
He went to hell only because he died

Soon the dead in hell will be raised
Death and hell no longer to be employed
For after the resurrection
Both death and hell will be destroyed

HAVE YOU EVER WONDERED WHY?

Have you ever wondered why
Times so critical are here
Why we must live each day of our lives
In dread and constant fear?

Have you ever wondered why
There's violence everywhere
For one another, for each his brother
Nobody seems to care?

Have you ever wondered why
So many are corrupt
From lawmakers to undertakers
From gospel preachers
To daycare teachers
Nobody can you trust?

Have you ever wondered why
There's always war and strife
Why so much love for money
So little value placed on life?

Have you ever wondered why
There's such selfishness and greed
Why those with plenty
Won't share with the many
Who have a real and urgent need?

Have you ever wondered why
There's such a lack of spirituality
Why injustice is the reality
And we abound in immorality?

Have you ever wondered why
Occultism is on the rise
Why drugs, devils and demons
Are what many seem to prize?

Well, the answer my friend
Is not in the wind
But in that we are living
IN THE TIME OF THE END.

TRUE HAPPINESS

Positive psychology states that
    the pathways leading to happiness are three,
Having a pleasant life, an engaged life
    and a meaningful life are what they are said to be

Traversing these roads may very well
    lead to happiness in a limited measure
But to find true happiness
    one must search as if for hidden treasure

True happiness is in deed
    one of life's greatest treasures
But true happiness comes not from
    the sampling of life's many pleasures

Losing oneself to some passion or activity
    does not true happiness bring
For, what if that passion or activity
    is bad and not a good thing?

Having a meaningful life means a lot
    but a road to true happiness, No, it is not
Many are the one's who have meaningful lives
    but then that's all they've got

True happiness comes only from <u>knowing</u>
    the Creator, "the Happy God" as the Bible states
And from knowing his Son, Jesus Christ
    called the "Happy and Only Potentate."

LOVE IS

Love is, according to the dictionary
    an intense affectionate concern for another
As for a friend, for a parent or child
    for a sister or for a brother

Love is, also, an intense sexual desire
    a desire for sex with someone you love
Not with some casual acquaintance
    some stranger, someone you know nothing of

Love is, a strong fondness or enthusiasm
    not just for a person but also for a place or thing
It can be a love for the out of doors,
    a love for the water, or just a love to sing

The best definition of love
    in the Bible you'll find
For in it love is described as
    enduring, patient, long suffering and kind

Love's greatest example is none other
    than our Great God above
He is its very personification
    Just as the Bible says, God IS Love

Chapter 2 AND THEN THERE IS LOVE

Probably nothing is talked about, written about or sung about more than love. This is very understandable when you consider the Bible's description of love. "Love is patient, love is kind. It does not envy, it does not boast, it is not proud. It is not rude, it is not self-seeking, it is not easily angered, it keeps no record of wrongs. Love does not delight in evil but, rejoices with the truth. It always protects, always trusts, always hopes, always perseveres. Love never fails.

DISTANT LOVERS

Love, O Love of Mine
Until again we meet
These lips long for yours so sweet
Here in my heart you'll always be
Evermore, eternally
Remember this always my sweet

While you're so far away
How hard it is for me to sleep
I shall survive somehow, I know my dear
Though, days and weeks must past before you are here
Love alone shall guide us when together are we again
Ecstasy once more will fill us
Yearning a returning never more to be our claim

AND THEN THERE IS LOVE

There are four letter words
There are more letter words
And then there is love

There are verbs and adverbs
To be or not to be
And then there is love

There are words that modify
Words that limit, specify or qualify
And then there is love

Other nouns are around
Some even quite profound
And then there is love

There are words with strength
Words with power
And then there is love

If all known words were mounted
One on top of the other
At the pinnacle there would be love

JUNE (A Song)

I once knew a girl named April
I once knew a girl named May
But the one for whom I wrote my tune
Was the lovely, the charming . . . June

The day that I first meet her
Is the day I fell in Love
For there is no other girl
In this whole wide world
Like the one for whom I wrote my tune
The lovely, the charming . . . June

She said that she was married
That she could never be mine
Friends we could be, platonically
The one for whom I wrote my tune
The lovely, the charming . . . June

Never will I forget her
She's always on my mine
I Love her still and I always will
The one for whom I wrote my tune
The lovely, the charming . . . June

FALLING IN LOVE

Why is there so much talk about
   Falling in love, being in love
Why is there so much prose and poetry about
   Falling in love, being in love
Why are there so many movies about
   Falling in love, being in love

Why do so many yearn to and dream of
   Falling in love, being in love
What is................so great about
   Falling in love, being in love
There is nothing, absolutely nothing like
   Falling in love, being in love

To fall in love, to be in love
   Is to live
And this is especially true
   When the one you have fallen in love with
   Has fallen in love with you

When you are in love
   You hear beautiful music all the time
You hear Brahms Bach, Beethoven, Schubert, Strauss
You hear Luther, Marvin, Teddy, Barry and Smokey

When you are in love
   Your eyes see continuous beauty
   They see Renoirs, Rembrandts, and Picassos
When you are in love

   Aromatic fragrances are what you smell
   Roses, lilacs, honeysuckles, apple blossoms

When you are in love
   Your palate is satisfied with your every
   Culinary delight

When you are in love
   Everything good touches you
   And everything you touch is good

When two lovers are in love
   They love not just each other's body
   But each other's mind, soul and spirit

Lovers love being in love
So what do lovers do?
   Lovers spend time together, as much as possible
   Lovers go out together
   Lovers stay in together
   Lovers love being together, it does not matter where

Lovers talk to each other
   They talk about silly things
   They talk about things deep and personal
Lovers support each other, building each other up
   They seek not their own interest but that of the other

Lovers laugh together, often laughing at each other
Lovers sometimes even cry together
   As when something touches them both

Anyone who asks what's so great about
    Falling in love, being in love
Must have never fallen in love, must
    Have never been in love
Because anyone who's ever fallen in
    Love, who has ever been in love
    Knows that there is <u>nothing</u> like
Falling in love, being in love.

SOMETHING BEAUTIFUL

What could be more beautiful than the growth of a plant
Not just any plant but a plant that you were given
because it was considered as good as dead.
A plant whose vital signs were almost impossible to find
A plant drooped over as if it were carrying
the weight of a mountain

A plant whose smile had turned upside-down into a frown
but you took the structure and nursed it back to life
Its soil you changed and rearranged, and with the best plant
food that money could buy, you fed it
Only purified water you gave it to drink

You talked to it, encouraged it, built it up,
told it how beautiful it was becoming
and how pleased you were with its progress
Your work with it was imbued with
the spirit of determination
Finally, one day you found it standing statuesque,
in all of its radiant glory
In the splendor of a plant, the leaves of which waxed poetic
about the magnificent job you had done.

You could hardly wait to see the giver of that plant
To tell them, to show them what had
become of the plant you had received DOA
What could be more beautiful than this story? Perhaps this.

A love affair involving two people
A love affair that was thought to be over
but was rekindled and nurtured and
it blossomed in the same way as this plant
with the same beautiful outcome.

THEY'RE NOT THE SAME

There are two phrases that
   people often interchange
They do this even though
   the phrases are not quite the same

Making love / Having sex
Making love / Having sex

Making love is sexual activity
   between <u>lovers</u>
People who care deeply for
   one another
People concerned foremost for
   the other's satisfaction
And not their own,
   in other words, to make love
   a couple must first be .... in love

While making love often involves
   embracing and caressing
And while tenderness is always
   on duty
Making love is not just getting
   physical
But also getting emotional, sometimes
   even spiritual

Having sex on the other hand, is different
having sex is purely physical
You can have sex with anybody
You can have sex with someone
You don't even know
You can have sex with someone
That you don't even like

It can be a casual acquaintance, a call girl,
street walker, a toy bought from a store
Most prostitutes have strict rules
get right to the business at hand
No foreplay and no kissing
but go straight to the promised land
Their business is not making love
but having sex
Dispatching each customer quickly
then on to the next

A friend once told me that she enjoyed
Just having sex. She said that not only
Did just having sex spell relief;
But also that having sex kept her going
Having sex kept her going
Kept her going
Until she could find someone,
Someone that she could <u>make love</u> with.

Chapter 3 THE MATING GAME

The survival of all species of living things depends on reproduction. If any species - human beings, dogs or tulips - stopped reproducing, it would disappear when its present members die off. Since human beings and most higher animals reproduce sexually this requires a mate of the opposite sex. The mating habits of some animals are quite interesting.

HOW THEY FIND A MATE

In the animal kingdom mates
    are often found
Not by sight but by
    their scent or their sound.

Some secrete a fluid so pungent
    it can be smelled for miles around
It says to the opposite sex: "I'm ready
    so come on down."

Other animals make weird, eerie mating calls,
    calls that say to suitors, "I'm all alone
    so come on over and if you believe in love
    let's get it on."

BUTTING HEADS

To mate, some animals
must win the right
and this comes only after
there's been a fight

When big horn sheep
come into rut
if they have any rivals
Then there heads must butt

I saw this on *"Animal Planet"*
It was kind of funny
Two rams butting heads
trying to win a gawking honey

Exhausted after butting
heads all day
Another ram came out the brush
and whisked that honey away.

THE PLIGHT OF AN ARACHNID

Got involved with a woman
    not long ago
She wanted to move real fast
    I wanted to take it slow
Right away she tried to get
    me in her bed
But I was trying not to
    lose my head
If it sounds like this woman is
    some kind of "ho"
The truth is that we're spiders
    and she's a black widow
I know that once we mate
    that will be the end of me
Not just cast aside
    but my head bitten off viciously
But what I had seen
    just the other day
One of my brothers get a "quickie"
    and then dash away
His escape, however, was only short-lived
    being over confident he tried it again
That's when she bit his head off
    that's when he met his end
I am, of course, in my prime
    would love to get some woman in bed
I wanna make love
    but I just don't want to lose my head.

A BALL OF FUN

When it
comes to animals mating
some snakes top them all. What
some do is wrap themselves up in
what is called a mating ball. As many
as a dozen males may wrap themselves
around one female. For hours, sometimes even days they do nothing at
all, nothing but whatever they do
wrapped up in that great
big ball.

WHY DOES THE FIREFLY FLASH?
(Or Why Does the Lighting Bug Light?)

On many early summer nights
   Fireflies literally fill the air
Flashing their lights in the night
   They appear to be everywhere

Why does the firefly flash?
   He is signaling to potential mates
For as he flashes, he also looks
   The right flash from a female he awaits

When he gets the right flash from a female
   he lights out after her making a mad dash
Determined to light up that female
   who gave him that flash.

HE UNDERSTANDS PREGNANCY

Something very strange and different
Happens when seahorses mate
It's not the female but the male
That starts to pick up weight

It's the male that gets pregnant
It's his body that must change
He is the one that gives birth
He goes through labor, he has the pain.

Chapter 4 THE DATING GAME

In western society dating is the customary way of acquiring a mate. Dating is meeting socially by appointment at a particular time, especially with a member of the opposite sex. It also refers to going exclusively with a particular person.

In earlier times such meetings required a chaperon, however, in modern society couples going out alone or staying in alone is no longer frowned upon. Moreover, dating today, is not primarily a way to find a marriage mate but a form of recreation. To take the "hassle" out of finding suitable dates, computerized dating services have been formed and have developed into a multibillion dollar business. Television and newspaper spots claiming to find a person the right match are quite popular.

NO DATING

In Bible times it did not exist
   there was no such thing as dating
When it came time to marry
   it was the parents who did the mating.

Now, before you begin to criticize
   there is something you must realize
That God's people had no problem with this
   as it was fine and acceptable in God's eyes.

What about God's people today?
Dating is a way to find a marriage mate.
   Because it's not a game, not recreation,
If not looking to marry then they don't date.

What's wrong with dating for fun
   dating for recreation
It's what dating most often leads to
   that sin called fornication.

IF IT SUITS THEM, FINE

In some cultures even today
    couples don't spend time alone
If they are to get together
    they must have a chaperon

In permissive western societies
    where almost anything goes
By the third date, max
    they're already out of their clothes

And any culture or society
    that doesn't view dating this way

They laugh at and ridicule
    about them having nothing good to say.

WHY I CAN NEVER BE, "JUST FRIENDS"
(Overheard from a Coworker)

When you're "just friends" with a woman
she will often call on . . . YOU
When her car breaks down and there is
no one else around she'll call on you
When she's lonely and blue not knowing
just what to do, she'll call on you
When she has no dollars and she needs a few
your phone will ring, she'll call on you
When the garbage disposer gets stuck
and she's out of luck, she'll call on you
When there is some place she wants to go
and everyone else says no, she'll call on you
When she's vexed and perplexed and doesn't know what to
do next, she'll call on you
When she hears scary noises in the middle of the night
filling her with fright, she'll call on you
Whatever, whenever, or wherever
she needs anything, she'll call on you
<u>BUT</u>, when she needs some loving
and you would gladly help
That's when she calls . . . somebody else.

Chapter 5 CAPITAL PUNISHMENT

Capital punishment is the most misunderstood penal practice in the world today. While death penalty opponents have some legitimate objections, the truth is that capital punishment was not man's idea but God's. Being from God the principle could not be bad. The problem with capital punishment is the criminal justice system. As misunderstood as capital punishment is there is something that is even more misunderstood: "Thou Shall Not Kill."

NOT PLAYING GOD

Executing murderers
Is not playing God
Executing murderers
Is obeying God

For it is God who
Long ago said
"Whoever sheds man's
Blood, by man will his
Blood be shed"

The way one feels
About capital punishment
I am compelled to mention
Is the way one feels about God
For capital punishment
Is His invention

DOES GOD GET UPSET?

When a murderer is executed
who gets upset?
Surely not God
and on this you can bet.

You see, the Scriptures
make it perfectly clear
that executing murderers
is not man's, but God's idea.

For it is God who long ago said,
"Whoever sheds man's blood,
by man will his blood be shed."

So, if executing murderers
makes you upset
then take it up with God
and see how far you get.

WHERE MURDERERS BELONG

The place for murderers,
Where should they be found?
Not alive in some prison
But quite dead, deep in the ground

If because of their conduct
This fate they've incurred
From committing more crimes
They have now been deterred

Since the best fertilizer
Comes from things rotten
When a murderer is executed
Good fertilizer you have gotten

DOES THE STATE HAVE THE RIGHT?

It has the power
It has the might
But to take a person's life
What gives the state the right?

It is God who gives the state the right,
This he did when he long ago said,
"Whoever sheds man's blood
By man will his blood be shed."

Although the state's conduct
At times may be quite sinister
In maintaining law and order
It acts as "God's minister."

This is the truth
And these are the facts
Lest you incur the state's wrath,
Stay away from criminal acts.

MURDERERS: USELESS PEOPLE

Of all the people on this earth,
Who are the ones who have no worth?
Who should not be allowed to live?
Who to society have nothing at all to give?
Who have committed such a heinous deed?
Who is it that execution is what they need?
Who but the murderer fits this bill?
Who but the murderer is it right to kill?

WHEN SHOULD MURDERERS BE FORGIVEN?

It is said that capital punishment denies
> the possibility of redemption and rehabilitation.

This is oh so very true
But then that's what capital punishment is supposed to do

The basis for forgiveness is that an offender must
> truly be sorry and must rectify the wrong

if he has taken money, he must pay it back
if he has taken a life, he must pay that back

So as soon as the murderer expresses remorse
> and brings his victim back to life

Then he will have been redeemed,
Then he will have been rehabilitated.

> Then he should be forgiven.

A TIME TO BE LEERY

There is one who is a murderer
He was caught, convicted and sent to jail
On death row he "found God" and was "born again."
But did he really find God?
Was he truly "born again?" Doubtful!
You see, if he had really "found God"
If he had truly been "born again"
Then he would have had no qualms about being executed
For, if he had really "found God"
If he had truly been "born again."
He would have known that he owed God a life
And so would have been ready to pay up
Ready to be executed.
That is if he had really "found God"
If he had truly been "born again."

A BIG DIFFERENCE

When I was a youngster
    I would hear people say it from time to time
But there was just something about it
It didn't sound quite right
When I would question them about it
    Their answers were always crippled
When I grew up
    I would hear it said from time to time
and there was still something about it
    It just didn't sound right
Even when I read it myself
    There was something about it
It didn't sound quite right
It was too concise, yet too broad
There was no qualification, no explanation
    Which is probably why it didn't sound right
Something was missing
Something was wrong

It was like that yummy looking sweet potato pie
One taste and you knew something was missing
You couldn't tell what it was at first
But your palate began to speak
And it kept saying: No nutmeg, no nutmeg
That's the way that old saying was
There was something about it
There was something wrong, something missing
It didn't sound quite right
Actually when the ramifications were considered

It really didn't make sense
Well, after some study and investigation
I found out why it didn't sound right
I found that it was not quite right

One wrong word
All of this time, all of these people
The wrong word
It has been corrected in most up to date publications
However, you still hear uncorrected ones
    unenlightened ones
those guilty of misapplication
those who don't have a clue as to what
they are saying........still making that
erroneous statement, still saying:
"Thou Shall Not Kill" when the correct
phrase is "Thou Shall Not Murder"

A BIG DIFFERENCE

"THOU SHALL NOT KILL"

Preaching "Thou Shall Not Kill,"
when is the right time?
Not at state executions, but
<u>Before</u> the murderer commits the crime

"Thou Shall Not Kill" was for the citizens
Not for the state
Not to prevent executions
But to stem the murder rate

The truth of the matter is
The correct rendering, if you will,
Is Thou Shall Not Murder
And not Thou Shall Not Kill

THE GUILTY PARTY

Who puts innocent people on death row?
    Not capital punishment.

Who is it that is racially biased?
    Not capital punishment.

Who is it that is immoral?
    Not capital punishment.

Who is it that is unjust?
    Not capital punishment.

Who then is guilty of all of these things?
    Not capital punishment.

It is the Criminal Justice System

Chapter 6 ABOUT CARS

Americans travel much more than citizens of other countries. The myth of Americans' love affair with our cars may actually be a marriage of convenience. Contemporary land-use patterns require the use of private vehicles, whether or not we love those vehicles. Americans own more vehicles than citizens of other countries. Figures from the 1995 Nationwide Personal Transportation Survey (NPTS) show approximately one vehicle for every one driver, and 1.78 vehicles per household. Not shown is the huge increase in SUVs, vans, and pickup trucks, which are increasingly used as household vehicles.

MISS ANN

Her first car was an old clunker
What might be called a hoopdy today
A bright yellow VW that she called Miss Ann
Boy, did she love Miss Ann
Didn't take good care of her
Drive her is all that she ever did
For nearly a year
She drove, and drove, and drove
And if you rode with her
You were praying all the while
For Miss Ann would often break down
Cars with good brakes were sometimes said
To be able to stop on a dime
Well not so for Miss Ann
She couldn't stop on a 50-cent piece
Her exhaust was black
There was a hole in her floor
The latch was broken, it had to be held
On the driver's side door
Finally came Inspection Day
She knew she hadn't taken care of Miss Ann
And as she drove to the Inspection Station
She was filled with fear and trepidation
When Miss Ann failed, she was not surprised
But what happened next brought tears to her eyes
They took Miss Ann away from her
Pasted a Big Red Sticker on the windshield that said
CONDEMNED
This vehicle is unsafe to drive.

BUDDY

My oldest brother was named James
But we called him Buddy
Didn't know why, never even wondered
Although he was four years older than me
Buddy and I were still buddies
We talked a lot, he taught me a lot
Buddy was the best big brother
That one could ever have
When I was seventeen, it was a very good year
One of the best years of my life
It was the year I met the girl around the corner
The girl who in time would become my wife
Something else happened that year
Buddy bought a brand-new car
A 1958 Mercury Monterey

It was a big roomy car with glass
all around. It was actually a luxury car
with a new feature
The gears were not shifted with a lever
They were not changed with a stick
Push buttons mounted right on the dash
They are what did the trick
Buddy did something that summer
Something that just blew me away
He let me drive him to work
And keep his car all day
His only demands were that I
Drive safely

And that I pick him up on time
If I were faithful in doing this
All day long the car would be mine

MR. WALKER'S INTERNATIONAL

Mr. Walker worked at night
On his way home he drove right by my house
Waited on the corner every Saturday morning
That is the day we sold wood,
From his 1937 International Harvester truck
It was a big yellow truck, filled with wood when we got there
It was already twenty years old, when I began working

But the only problem we ever had with it
Was getting it started sometimes
I would often have to lay on the running board
Pouring gas into the carburetor as Mr. Walker
Would crank it up
Once we got the truck started, there was no stopping us
The wood was piled like a mountain on
The truck, dangerously high
It was mostly wood from demolished houses
That had only been cross cut.
So atop that pile I had to split
The wood, put it into bushel baskets
As Mr. Walker drove along shouting, Wood!
My only thoughts were of selling wood
Not because I was paid a commission
But because I was deathly afraid and
My only concern was getting that mound down
After about the first hour I was fine
Very much relieved as Mr. Walker continued
Driving and shouting, Wood!

Chapter 7 ABOUT PEOPLE

While many humans love watching animals because there are so many kinds, with so many peculiar looks, habits, and idiosyncracies that it is just mind boggling. If animals could talk I am sure that they would say, that people are some strange characters. Well, I can talk and I'm here to testify that people are indeed some strange, but interesting characters. You have to love them though.

LAZY PEOPLE ARE CRAZY PEOPLE

To show that this saying
Is true
This is the kind of thing
That lazy people will do
They will quit their job
On the silliest whim
Then have the nerve to ask
If you'll take care of them

You take a lazy person in
To help them get on their feet
What do they do, never go job hunting
Just sit before your TV and eat
If you say something to them
What I've found to be characteristic
That they'll turn on you
Saying things like you're too materialistic

You find them a good job
But they quit it too
Offering this as an excuse
"Supervisor was always telling me what to do"
They make ridiculous excuses
For why they are so slack
I would go to work but my car was repossessed
And I'm afraid I'll get car-jacked
To lazy people, the crazy people
Are not those who shirk
But the ones who don't mind
Doing their share of any kind of work.

WHO'S YOUR DADDY?

My daddy is coming home soon
My sister would say
My daddy is coming home soon
Maybe tomorrow, maybe even today.

I don't know where your daddy is
She would say to me
I don't know where your daddy is
Don't know where he could be.

When her daddy did come home
I found this to be true
When her daddy did come home
I found that he was my daddy too.

At the time that I was born
He was not on hand
At the time that I was born
He was in the Air Force in some distant land.

When I first met my dad
Didn't know just what to do
When I first met my dad
My sister was four and I was two.

KATRINA, KATRINA

When it comes to mean women
I have met a few
But I have never met anyone who was
Meaner than Katrina

Katrina was mean
The meanest woman I've ever seen
Katrina was huge. A huge woman
With a big bellowing voice

And when she spoke, she spoke with
A force that could literally blow you away
And boy did Katrina have something to say
She engage in a tirade for days

I had heard that she was coming
But like so many others, I said
I ain't scared of no Katrina
I had met some mean women before
I had met Camille who was for real
And so I regarded Katrina as no big deal

Bring on Katrina, bring her on is what I said
You know that old saying: Be careful of what
You ask for because you just might get it.
Well when Katrina came, I got it, he, she, and it got it;
We got it, you got it and they got it.
Anything, or anybody in her way, got it

Katrina was equal opportunity, she gave everybody some
She did not discriminate.

Looking back on Katrina, the only thing
That I can say is that Katrina must
Have had children......because Katrina was a Motha.

MOTHER'S, NO

My father's answers were always, no
Would have to go to mother to get a yes
Didn't matter what dad was asked it was always, no
Didn't matter what mother was asked, it was always, yes
Mother would never tell us no, sent us to dad to get his, no

SUBTERRANEAN MAN

He could hear the old bed squeak,
Started out slowly

Squeak..............squeak.....................squeak

The squeaks then multiplied and intensified

And after reaching a crescendo, they died

He could tell when his wife's
New lover paid a visit

For when their marriage broke up
Neither moved out, she stayed upstairs

He moved to the basement

MOTHER'S PRIZED POSSESSION

Found on the west side
It was old, very old
It put you to mind of an
Old person whose bones
Had become brittle
And whose flesh was shriveled
On those bones

It was one of the things mother loved
It was one of her prized possessions
She treated it like a person
Forbade us to touch it
Ordered us to never go near it

One day I looked up and I couldn't
Believe my eyes
Emma, my sister, was swinging on one of its limbs
Before I could yell, something went c-r-a-c-k
Emma fell to the ground, still clutching
The limb of mother's prized cherry tree

Immediately tears filled her eyes
Crying, she began questioning me, begging, pleading
Can you get a hammer and nails, and nail it back up?
She knew she was in for it
With a hammer and nails, I got it up
But I knew there would soon come a day
When the slightest wind would bring it down again
And we would both have to pay

She got hers for swinging on mother's
Cherished cherry tree
I got mine for not telling
And for being an accessory

SPOILED SODA?

After asking for the rest of that red
soda in that bottle in the refrigerator

They got two glasses, poured some
in each, all the while measuring

To ensure that the glasses were each
filled to the same level

I need a little bit more in mine
one would say

Only when they agreed that both glasses
were at exactly the same level
did either dare to raise their glass

They both took a sip at the same time and
they both exclaimed, this soda is spoiled!

I never found out how it got into the refrigerator
what I'm talking about is the remainder
of that transmission fluid that I poured
from a can into a soda bottle because
the bottle had a cap.

UM UM GOOD

On the outside they were always
Brown and crispy

On the inside they were
Always light and airy

Never thick and gooey
That is how dad's waffles always were
Um, um good

GOOD PANCAKES

To make good pancakes
You can't use just any ole mix
The best results comes from a
Blend of flours that you fix

Rule number two, once you pour the batter
On a lightly greased griddle
And after the bubbles have appeared
With the cakes you cannot fiddle
You touch them only twice

Once to turn them over

And once to take them off

SOMETHING NICE

Frantically she searched her room
Like the police armed with a warrant
Searching the drawers, tossing its contents
Finally she exclaimed, "it was right here
on my dresser, and now its gone!

Has anybody seen my diamond bracelet?
Mother, dad, have you seen my diamond bracelet?
To her younger brother I heard her say
"Donny, come here right away
Have you seen my diamond bracelet?
It was right here on my dresser,
Did you take it?"

She didn't have to ask twice
That look on his face gave him away
What did you do with it?
I took it to school!
For show and tell she asked
No, I gave it to Kate

Who is Kate? Kate is my classmate.
Why did you give her my bracelet?
She's pretty, I like her and I wanted
To give her something nice
And I don't have anything nice
How old is this Kate? She's seven just like me
Mother, dad come here please
Donny gave my bracelet to his girlfriend

Because she's pretty and he wanted to
Give her something nice

Wanting to hear it from him, mother asked,
"Did you take your sister's bracelet to
School and give it away?"
He opened his mouth and said yes, knowing
That head signals were not permitted

Mother was able to find Kate's mother from
The phone book
Kate brought the bracelet to school and Donny
brought the bracelet back home
Needless to say, Joanne was a happy camper

MY FAVORITE DRINK

Fresh out of the military
Couldn't wait to get back home
For two years I had longed
For my favorite drink

Stopped at a corner store
Got two of my favorite drinks
Took one swig and spat it out
Colored water!

Poor quality control I surmised
Tried several other stores
Same result
Finally I read the label

Discovered that a new bottler
Was now producing my favorite drink
Realized that they had turned
My favorite delicious grape soda
Into mere purple colored carbonated water

THAT WOMAN (A Song)

There is a woman on my job
She's as fine as she can be
All the guys go crazy over her
But the one she wants is me

She always tries to catch me in
The office all alone
But I duck and dodge and keep away
I've got a lovely wife at home

One snowy winter day is when
I really got my test
Only she and I showed up for work
It was a sin how she was dressed

When she took off her fancy coat
About the only thing I can say
Is that what she had for a dress
Looked more like lingerie

She danced and pranced
And flirted all around
Doing all she could to
Wear my resistance down

Just when I thought
I couldn't hold out anymore
Something came to mind,
Something I had studied not too long ago

It was about a man named Joseph
And his boss's wife
When she tried to seduce him
He left his garment in her hand, running for his life

That's when I took off
Running across the floor
When I heard her call my name
I was already out the door

The moral of this story
Be strong if you can
And that a goo run
Is always better than a bad stand

SLEEPING BEAUTY

Never saw anyone sleep so
Peacefully in a chair

No bobbing or weaving at all
Wake him up I didn't dare

The boss said, "I'm sure
He must be very tired

So, as long as he's asleep he's got a job
But once he wakes up, tell him he's fired."

TO BE A POET

The ability to make one's words rhyme
All of the time only makes one a rhymer

The ability to pen and spout
Obscenities and vulgarities
Does not one a poet make

But the ability to perceive and express
The beautiful, or lyrical
To be a poet, does it take

Chapter 8 PHILOSOPHY

The American Heritage Dictionary lists twelve definitions of Philosophy. The one that I like is number eleven, which says: The system of values by which one lives.

THE HYPOCRISY OF DEMOCRACY

They say that with democracy
Everyone has a voice
But unless you're with the majority
You really don't have a choice
That's the hypocrisy of democracy

Democracy, to be sure
Is highly overrated
Especially is this true when democracy
And justice are somehow equated
That's the hypocrisy of democracy

They say, "get out and vote"
That's the way to make a change
And if you don't vote
You have no right to complain
That's the hypocrisy of democracy

Many flock to the polls
And it's just a doggone shame
That after exercising their "sacred duty"
They do nothing but complain
That's the hypocrisy of democracy

The best form of government
Democracy is said to be
Better than any other
Embrace it, it will set you free
Ah, the hypocrisy of democracy

For those who like to brag
Just look around
Racism, injustice, poverty, war, crime
In democracies these things are also found
The hypocrisy of democracy

What's wrong with democracy?
It's what democracy purports to be
The solution to mankind's government
A God sent remedy
That's the hypocrisy of democracy

A better form of government
This earth is soon to see
One that will end all war, crime and violence
<u>Really</u> set mankind free
Not democracy, but Theocracy

This government will wipe away all tears
Do away with sickness, disease, and death
It will raise the dead until
Nobody in the grave is left
Not democracy, but Theocracy

Theocracy is rule by God
The way it's supposed to be
Man could never rule himself
For he lacks the ability
Theocracy, not democracy

Just like monarchies and hierarchies,
Democracy too will fall
Totalitarian, dictatorial, communistic
God will eliminate them all
Theocracy, not democracy

As earth's new leader, Jesus will be installed
"Joy to the world" is what his rule will bring
"Joy to the world" the Lord now reigns
Let earth receive her king
Theocracy, not democracy

STOP THE BITCHIN'

I am tired of hearing people constantly complaining,
griping, bitchin'
Bitchin' about this and bitchin' about that
Bitchin' about politicians
The president promised this or he didn't do that
Presidents are politicians and politicians are liars and
cheaters (that's what they do)
Some do it better than others and so they don't get caught
But they are still politicians and "politicians are all alike
No matter what the color of their stripes"
Republicans, Democrats, Independents, they're all the same
Politicians called by different names.
Politicians are like wolves in sheep's covering
They are out to get you
And they will promise anything to get in office
They cannot fulfill all of those promises
You know this
So stop the bitchin'

Everybody bitches about their job
My job this and my job that
Bitchin' about one's job seems to be, SOP
People bitch about how little money they make
They bitch about how many hours they work
How hard they work
They bitch about not getting promoted,
 About coworkers and supervisors

Remember, bitchin' is like frowning
And it takes more energy to frown than to smile
So find something on your job to smile about
And stop the bitchin'

Blacks.......bitch about whites
The white man this and the white man that
Some blacks blame everything on race
The wife says, "no honey, not tonight I have a headache"
It's the white man's fault

Junior gets an "F" in Biology
It's the white mans faults.

It's true, racism is still alive and kicking in America
But it is not kicking as high as it once did
Still blacks, should never forget their heritage
They should never forget the atrocities
They should never become complacent
But this is a new day
Blacks, you control your own destiny
Blacks, you can now be all that you want to be
And if you don't like the situation
Then do something about it
Only..... stop the bitchin'

Remember Rosa Parks, she wasn't always bitchin'
Martin Luther King didn't sit around bitchin'
Thurgood Marshall, you didn't hear him bitchin'
Johnnie Cochran wasn't known for bitchin'
Again, if you don't like the situation

Then do something about it
Just stop the bitchin'

Some bitch about the police
The police do this and the police do that
They say, "when you don't need them
They're always around
But when you really want them
Not a single one can be found."

When the police shoot the teenager
Who was pointing a gun at them, they bitch
"They didn't have to shoot him so many times"
When they get at ticket for driving 60
In a 25-mile zone, they bitch
"He should have been out catching bank robbers"
Or, "that other car was going faster than I was"
Would you like it if we had no police, no?
So stop the bitchin'

Women bitch about men
Those who don't have a man, bitch
They say all men are dogs
A good man is hard to find
I can do bad by myself

Those who do have a man bitch even worse
My man doesn't do this, or
He doesn't do that
He doesn't talk unless he wants sex
Always rough, never gentle

My birthday and our anniversary
He never remembers
He never picks up after himself
What can I do?

You can either train him
Or continue treating him as you would
Like him to treat you
Constantly complaining to your girlfriends
Won't help
So stop the bitchin'

Men bitch about women
Women get on my nerves
They always want to talk
You can't live with them and can't live without them

I just don't understand women
Why can't they think like men?
They're not supposed to think like men
They're women

And you are not supposed to understand them
They don't understand themselves sometimes
All you have to do is just love them
And be good to them
You want to make your woman happy
And keep her happy?
Pay attention to your woman,
Take notice of her.

Be observant.
Notice her hair, her clothes
The expressions on her face
Observe everything about her and around her

Remember these things, comment on them
Talk to your lady
Listen to your lady
Find out the things she likes

Do some of them
Find out what turns her on
And turn her on regularly

Women are like flowers - they want attention
Give it to them and they blossom
So just do it
And stop the bitchin'

Parents bitch about their children
"My kids won't do this or they won't do that
These kids just get on my nerves
I need to get away for a while"

Children act the way they're trained to act
Who trains them? Parents
Either actively or passively
So, if you've got bad kids
You've probably got yourself to blame
So stop the bitchin'

Children bitch about their parents
My parents this or my parents that
They don't understand young people
Too many stupid rules

Young ones, your parents love you
They want the best for you
Your parents are your guardians
Put in charge of you by God
So be obedient to them
Be respectful, God commands this

Remember, youth is not going to last forever
Before you know it you're going to
Be an adult with all of the cares
And worries of adulthood

In the meantime, try to learn as much as you can
And have as much fun as you can
And above all, stop the bitchin'

Whites..... bitch about blacks
Black people this and black people that
"I'm not a racist," they say, but "why can't blacks
be more like us?"

Why are so many lazy and shiftless?
Why do they always have so many children?
Why do they commit so much crime?
Why do they want to move into our neighborhoods
Lowering our property values?

These things are true of some blacks,
But they are also true of some whites
There is a saying "you reap what you sew"
Whites, you are reaping what you have sewn
Blacks were brought here by whites, misused
And abused for 400 years down to this very day

If blacks had been allowed an education long ago
If they had been treated decently and respectfully
Then some of the problems of today wouldn't exist
So stop the bitchin'

Finally, if you have a beef with the police
With anybody, with a store, with your whore
Your friend, your lover, your boss, even the
President and you can't meet them face-to-face

Then write them a letter
The keyboard is mightier than the sword
Also, there is something you should always remember
Something you should never forget

And that is..... that you are always
A part of the problem
Unless you are part of the solution
So just stop the bitchin'

CANCEL THAT SUBSCRIPTION

Do you subscribe to any *isms*, I-S-M
You know those 3 letters at the end of some words
Letters that tend to make good words bad
Letters that make bad words even worse
Some good words gone bad:

National – *ism*
The worship of ones nation
Rac – *ism*
The worship of ones race
Sex – *ism*
The worship of one's gender

If you subscribe to any of these *isms*
You might want to cancel that subscription
Or at least, let it lapse.

THE VANITY OF PROFANITY

Vanity is defined as: a lack of
Usefulness, no good, useless,
Worthless, vain
This makes it easy to see the vanity of profanity

It has been said, "for everything
There is a time and a season"
Profanity is most often used
At both the wrong time and for the wrong reason
That's the vanity of profanity

Some folks use profanity because
They know few other words
Some use profanity because
That's all they have ever heard
That's the vanity of profanity

Some use profanity because they think its cool
Some use it because they think its hip
Some just don't give a (kitty)
What kind of language escapes their lips?
That's the vanity of profanity

Some use it for emphasis
Some use it for spice
But no matter when or why it's used
It is almost never ever nice
That's the vanity of profanity

Some use profanity because
Of English they have no command
With others, it just a bad habit
It's not something they plan
That's the vanity of profanity

Enough about profanity
Someone will surely say
There are a lot worse habits
That we endure every day
That's the vanity of profanity

There are times, known by a few
That just happens to be
A time when the most ideal word
Is one of profanity?
That's the vanity of profanity

Once it has been uttered
The profanity you cannot recall
So to merely say, "Pardon my French"
Doesn't really help at all
That's the vanity of profanity

Some don't understand that profanity
Is not adult language?
Profanity is profane (vulgar) language
Language still hurtful to many ears
That's the vanity of profanity

THE GREATEST NATION

The greatest nation is the one where
    growth and prosperity literally abound

It is the one where hurtful things like
    crime and violence are almost never found

The greatest nation is a spiritual one
    a nation that is good to the core

Its citizens have real love for one another
    have vowed to study war no more

The leaders of this nation do not lord it
    over the citizens and are not known for politics

They are all scripturally qualified
    and don't engage in shady deals or dirty tricks

Citizens of this nation never brag or boast
    they are always humble, meek and kind

They never look down upon or belittle others
    some of the best folks that you could ever find

This nation was built by God
    It is real, no utopian dream

By those with spiritual discernment
    this nation can be seen.

EXPANSION
(For Gerri on Receiving Her Degree)

Expanding is something we do
All of the time
But the best kind of expansion
Is not of the body
But that of the mind

To school, to professors, to books
You've devoted much time
For but one lofty purpose, one noble goal
To that of expanding your mind

Now that you gotten your Masters
Now that you've earned your prize
It is my sincerest hope
That your hat remains the same size

A LITTLE MORE OF THE BEAUTIFUL, PLEASE

To hear beautiful words about beautiful things
Is why I came to the poets den
To hear those beautiful expressions
Written by the poet's pen

I came to hear about the majestic mountains
The mighty oceans and the seven seas
I came to hear about the sun, moon, and stars
About flowers, trees, and leaves

I came to hear about love, joy, and peace
About kindness, goodness, and self-control
I came to hear about all of beautiful things
That poets are said to extol

I came not to hear unbridled profanity,
I came not to hear wholesale filth and sleaze
And so humbly I ask
A little more of the beautiful, please

Chapter 9   A GUY THING

Because of the differences of the sexes, there are certain things that women relate to (girl things) and there are certain men things that only another man can relate to (guy things).

WITH WHAT DO YOU THINK?

It has been said that of our brains
We use maybe about 10 percent
Well, for many men that figure
Is more like some milk, 2 percent

For with many men
The brain in their head is dead
They use nothing cerebral
But the brain in their groin instead

MY FAVORITE THINGS

Hammers
Nails
Drills
Bits
Screw drivers
Screws
Lumber
Saws
Sheet rock
Joint compound
Tape measures
Squares
Levels
Faucets that leak
Floors that squeak
These are a few of my favorite things
For I am a handyman

NO BRAINER

While God endowed man with
A great sexual drive
He did this not solely for man's pleasure
But to keep the human race alive

For man to do his thinking
God put a brain in his head
He put no brain in the groin
For man to use instead

Men who think only with their members
Are destined for misery
This is not mere speculation
Just check your history

MY ULTIMATE HIGH

Never drank alcohol
Never did drugs
But I got high
Boy, did I get high
It has happened only once
My ultimate high
Early in my marriage
We made love once
That was so exhilarating,
So blissful that I felt
The sensation that night
And all of the next day
And part of the day after that
For nearly three days
I was on cloud nine
Needless to say that like
Someone on drugs I
Have been continuously
Pursuing that ultimate high.

I KNOW WHERE I AM

Took a little trip
To see a friend of mine
Two hundred miles or so
Three, maybe four hours driving time

He gave me good directions
But what I would soon learn
I seem to be going around in circles
Somehow made a wrong turn

That dilapidated old red barn
I know I past before
And that green and white cow
I know for sure

The needle is almost on "E"
And you know what gas cost
Been driving now for six hours
But guess what, I'm not lost

Chapter 10 ABOUT GUNS

America leads the world in gun possession. The U.S. Constitution give Americans the right to bear arms and bear arms they do. The National Institute of Justice (NIJ) reported in a National Survey that in 1994, 44 million people, approximately 35 percent of households, owned 192 million firearms, 65 million of which were handguns. Seventy-four percent of those individuals were reported to own more than one firearm. The Bureau of Alcohol, Tobacco and Firearms (ATF) estimates that as of the end of 1996, approximately 242 million firearms were available for sale to or were possessed by civilians in the United States. That total includes roughly 72 million handguns (mostly pistols, revolvers and derringers), 76 millions rifles, and 64 million shotguns.

IN GUNS WE TRUST

The gun is my shepherd, having it
I shall not be in want.
It makes me able to lie down
in peace, and security
as though by still waters.
Having it makes me feel good
for I am upholding an American tradition
my constitutional right.
Even though we live in
critical times, hard to deal with,
I will fear no evil
for my gun is with me.
It and these bullets
they comfort me.
Surely the blessing of the NRA will
follow me
all the days of my life
and I will dwell with my gun
which is my God, forever.

AMERICANS LOVE GUNS

Americans love guns
It's sad but it's true
Because they love guns
do they love killing too?

They say they amass guns
for hunting and sport
but killing each other
is to what many resort

Tell me please,
in the name of heaven
what kind of hunting
is done with an A.K. 47

Guns are for protection
at least that's what they say
but how many children and
elderly are killed everyday

They justify this insanity
with their favorite position,
"the right to bear arms"
is an American tradition.

QUICK DRAW

Eighteen years old, fresh out of high school
Airmen in the U.S. Air Force

We had sworn an oath declaring ourselves
to be American fighting men

The truth is we were still boys
Young, dumb and concerned only
With having fun

Armed with 30. caliber carbines and 45. caliber automatics
We often played "quick draw"

45's were some dangerous weapons
Like hand-held cannons

One day someone said something I didn't like
Before they knew it, my 45 was
Pressing on their chest

Before I could say, take it back
my finger accidentally pulled the trigger

Boom! is what I should have heard
But the gun misfired
I never played quick draw again.

Chapter 11 PROVERBIAL SAYINGS

"Proverbial sayings" is a Biblical expression. The term translated "proverbial saying" in Hebrew is generally thought to be derived from the root word meaning "to be like." This is understandable since many proverbial sayings employ likenesses or comparisons. Some scholars relate the expression "proverbial sayings" to the verb "to rule"; in doing this, it could be construed at times to be a saying of a ruler, an expression carrying power or one that indicates mental superiority. King Solomon aptly fits this picture for he was known for his wisdom and could speak three thousands proverbs. The Bible records many of his proverbial sayings, many in the book of Proverbs.

If proverbial sayings were peculiar to wise men especially wise rulers, how does the ordinary man qualify to know and speak proverbial sayings? Almighty God and Jesus Christ are the two great masters of proverbial sayings and so the ordinary man would certainly have to study them. Solomon, in Proverbs Chapter 1, also explains how the ordinary man could learn and utter proverbial sayings, verses one through six reads: "The proverbs of Solomon, son of David and king of Israel. Here are proverbs that will help you recognize wisdom and good advice, and understand sayings with deep meaning. They can teach you how to live intelligently and how to be honest, just, and fair. They can make an inexperienced person clever and teach young people how to be resourceful. These proverbs can even add to the knowledge of the wise and give guidance to the educated, so that they can understand the hidden meanings of proverbs and the problems that the wise raise."

There was a popular song not long ago that talked about two lovers who were said to not know which way to go. And why did they not know which way to go, according to the song? It was because they were "Just Ordinary People." The notion that ordinary people are lacking is not new. The rulers and religious leaders in Jerusalem were astonished at Peter and John for their boldness in declaring the good news about Jesus Christ. They were astonished because they perceived Peter and John to be unschooled and "ordinary." What they didn't understand is that God doesn't put a premium on higher education. The truth is that God favors ordinary people. Highly educated people are sometimes proud and haughty. They tend to rely on their knowledge and understanding whereas Proverbs say, "Trust in the Lord with all your heart and lean not on your own understanding."

It is therefore not surprising what Paul said: "So then, where does that leave the wise? Or the scholars? Or the skillful debaters of this world" God has shown that this world's wisdom is foolishness.

Now remember what you were my friends, when God called you. From the human point of view, few of you were wise or powerful or of high social understanding. God purposely chose what the world considers nonsense in order to shame the wise, and he chose what the world considers weak in order to shame the powerful. He chose what the world looks down on and despises and thinks is nothing, in order to destroy what the world thinks is important." 1 Corinthians 1:20, 26-28

So it is "ordinary" people that God empowers and employs to do his work. Thus, "ordinary" people who speak God's wisdom can also utter proverbial sayings.

GOD

For God to be nameless would be like his son, Jesus being nameless.

•

Some say that God's name should not be used because we are not sure of the correct pronunciation. They nevertheless pronounce most everything else incorrectly.

•

Not all are God's children. For just as God has his children, so likewise the Devil has his children.

•

Do not worship the place where you live, but the one who allows you to live not in just that place but anywhere.

•

There are two kinds of soldiers: Soldiers in God's army, and then soldiers in the armies of the nations.
You cannot be a soldier in the army of any nation and a soldier in God's army too.

Never oppose the truth, for he who opposes the truth opposes God.

•

If you cannot think for yourself, then let God do your thinking. Read his Word daily, be guided by it.

•

All life belongs to God. Anyone taking the life of another owes God a life. There is only one way that a murderer can pay God a life and that is by his own life being taken by the duly constituted authority.

•

To ensure that the earth would be populated, God endowed women with a strong desire to have children and men with a strong desire to have sex.

•

You can fool your friends some of the time, you can fool your enemies some of the time, but you fool God, none of the time.

Certainly if torture and torment are considered inhumane, then they must also be ungodly, or are humans more compassionate than God?

THE BIBLE
A college education equips one for a career in this world. Bible education equips one for life in this world, as well as, for life in the world to come.

•

Customs and traditions are like any other kind of conduct. It matters not how old a custom or tradition is, but whether it adheres to godly principles.

•

When a man loves a woman, that's when he's got it right.
"Will leave his father and mother, and be united to his wife."

•

Drinking is not wrong when done in moderation. Drinking is wrong when it results in inebriation.

•

God says that it is okay to spank a child - are you smarter than God?

•

The true God puts before his worshipers only everlasting life or everlasting death. If your God tortures and torments, then you've got the wrong God.

•

Fornication, a sin against one's body is a sin just looking for a place to happen.

•

Do not put your hope and trust in ordinary men. Neither in world leaders. Especially not in world leaders. For they cannot save even themselves. Just like you, they too get sick, grow old, and die. What is more, they are inspired by the evil god of this world.

What only does the Christian owe his country? Not worship or sacred service, but only taxes and obedience to all laws that do not conflict with God's Law.

•

Intelligent people love intelligent discussions. Capital punishment cannot be discussed intelligently with anyone who uses the phrase, "Thou Shall Not Kill" because "Thou Shall Not Kill" is neither an intelligent nor correct saying. The correct saying is "Thou Shall Not Murder."

•

The forbidden fruit was not sex. God told Adam and Eve that they could and should have sex. He did this when he told them to be fruitful and multiply and fill the earth. Humans reproduce only through sex. Think God didn't know that?

You cannot go wrong when you go aright by the Bible.

•

Always be leery if you hear "voices." Be leery of others who hear "voices." God speaks by means of his written Word.

KNOWLEDGE AND WISDOM

He who knows and knows that he knows, and who makes good use of what he knows is wise. But he who knows not and, knows not that he knows not, and who will listen not, is foolish.

•

True wisdom is not a possession of all persons, for true wisdom starts with knowing the True God.

•

A mild answer to someone in a heated rage often has a calming effect.

•

A person not knowing God's Truth is a person blind and in slavery.

It is better to have modest provisions in a happy home than a house of plenty along with bitterness and contention.

•

A wise person ponders his actions - Controls his reactions.

•

A wise person doesn't have to experience everything for himself, but learns from the experiences of others.

•

Appreciation is but a mere token when it is not shown but only spoken.

•

A reasonable person limits the amount he puts on his plate - His plate of activity as well as his dinner plate.

•

When you must counsel someone, always start with commendation for doing this leads to greater appreciation.

Men, be good to your lady and she'll always remember it. Be mean to her and she'll never forget it.

•

Becoming a Christian doesn't mean donning a label but embracing a way of life.

•

One may have studied at a prestigious college or university, graduated high in his class, had conferred upon him a degree in an art or science and yet, if he doesn't know God's Truth, he has only been to kindergarten.

•

Higher learning upstairs is fine, provided there is common sense and godly wisdom on the ground floor.

•

Some folks talk too much. A good time to be quiet is when what you have to say is neither pertinent, positive nor profound.

Most people worship what they think. Those having God's Truth worship what they know.

•

A wise person is slow to anger but quick to forgive.

•

Just as a fire goes out when no fuel is added. A quarrel will also end when one side stop arguing.

•

Do not imitate stupid people who pose foolish questions to try to make you look foolish. Answer them only in a way that shows that you understand their foolish intent.

•

There will come a time in life when one will have to contemplate old age and death. Dreaded things to contemplate when one doesn't know God's truth.

•

One knowing God's Truth is able to cope with the madness of this world with joy and peace of mind.

GOD'S MINISTERS

The true man of God is not a glory seeker, doesn't want popularity for himself, but popularity for God.

•

Soldiers in God's army unlike soldiers in the armies of the nations, do not wage carnal warfare.

•

Neither natural ability nor educational advantage figure as big factors in being a minister of God. A willingness to be used by him is more important for God adequately equips those whom he uses.

•

Like Peter, a true minister of God will not allow other humans to bow down to him.

•

How can you often tell a minister of God, from a church minister? Whereas a minister of God will look like and ordinary person, a church minister will often look like a church minister.

•

True Christians are first and foremost . . . Christians. They are not defined by where they happen to live.

•

A true minister of God makes God's name known, makes God's name popular and not his own.

•

The true man of God is more like an ant than an elephant for he considers all others as superior to him.

•

The true person of God loves talking about his God, not himself.

•

The true man of God is rarely great or famous. Usually just an ordinary man.

•

The true man of God is not a fleshly man but a spiritual man and therefore he doesn't think about sex all the time.

•

Like Jesus, the true minister of God, doesn't call undue attention to himself by wearing distinctive religious garb, flashy clothes or by the use of self-elevating titles.

•

True Christians are a united brotherhood. They do not fight or kill one another.

CHURCH MINISTERS

A degree from a college or university, may make one a minister of his Church but it doesn't make one a minister of God.

•

A minister who has acquired a name for him is a celebrity and celebrities often suffer from vanity. Prominence belongs to God.

•

Church ministers are qualified by their churches. Ministers of God are adequately qualified by God.

Accepting religious titles only means that one thinks more of himself than God does.

•

Just as God has his ministers so likewise Satan has his ministers. Be on the watch, for Satan's ministers often masquerade as ministers of God.

•

Any Church minister who has to resort to theatrical spectacles, freak shows, hip hop music or other similar enticements to get people to his Church has a big big problem.

•

One's worship of God is in vain, a waste of time, when one's Church follows the bad practice mentioned by Jesus "Teaching as their doctrine the precepts of men."

FOOLISH ONES

Who is the stupid one? Anyone who fashions, builds or constructs his own god.

•

Who is the stupid one? Anyone who bows down in worship to an idol or image or who uses idols and images as aids in worship.

•

Who is the one who throws up barriers in his own mind to justify himself in not starting on a project? Who is the one who makes ridiculous excuses for his slothfulness?

Who is the one who has no respect for his fellow man? Who will try to get his fellow to do his work for him and even provide him with the things he desires?

Who but the lazy person fits this bill, thus verifying the saying that "lazy people are crazy people."

•

Illicit drugs defile the mind and body, turns smart people stupid.

Smoking defiles the body and you cannot defile your body with impunity.

•

He or she who smokes is like one who takes poison.

•

You can always reason with someone who is merely ignorant but you can never reason with a fool.

DEATH

Live your life as one with hope in the resurrection, as one who knows what death really is, as one who knows the true condition of the dead. That when you die you have nothing at all, that there is no knowledge, no wisdom, no conscious thought, no feelings in death, that torture and torment are not possible after death.

Death is not a change in life nor a transferral of life but the complete end of life. Death is an unconscious condition like sleep but without dreams. The dead are awakened only through the resurrection. The dead are alive only in someone else's memory, hopefully, in God's memory.

•

If the dead are somehow, someway still alive (other than in someone's memory) then the resurrection is rendered null and void.

•

For those prone to violence, regarding the sanctity of life the number one rule is: if you cannot bring it back then don't take it away.

•

Why are the ones so vehemently opposed to capital punishment so quiet on the alarming murder rate? Why do they have so much compassion for unremorseful convicted murderers but little or no compassion for the victim or his survivors?

It could not be that they have such great respect for

the sanctity of life, otherwise, they would not be so nonchalant about murder.

Could it be that their sense of moral value is misplaced or is it that capital punishment has such a bad image making it easy to oppose?

Or could it be that capital punishment is simply something convenient to protest?

•

It is the living that we should fear. Do not be in fear of the dead for the dead never murder, rob, rape or plunder.

•

Just as a person before he is conceived does not exist, so likewise, when he dies he no longer exists. That's why there's the Resurrection.

WORLDLY PERSONS
Not everyone professing Jesus as their Lord will be recognized by Him. Even some who will have performed wondrous acts and feats he will not own. For some will say just as it is written: "In your name we drove out many demons and performed many miracles!" Then I will say to them, "I never knew you. Get away from me, you wicked people."

•

Some who contend that they believe in God and then country will often become violently upset when someone belittles their country but only mildly upset if at all; when someone belittles their God.

•

The worldly person asks what he can do for his country? The spiritual person seeks to know what God wants of him.

•

A person of God does the things of God. A person of the world does worldly things. This is only unclear to those of the world.

•

Politics is a dirty business. Not a job for godly people. Excellent for worldly people.

INTEGRITY

If you resist when someone undeserving seeks your virtue - what do you do when your country asks from you that which only God is entitled to?

•

A captive audience is entitled to respect. Having a captive audience is not a license to use profanity or vulgarity.

•

A real man treats women real good.

Many are the ones who say "I'm blessed." But is one blessed simply because he says he's blessed? To be blessed is to be favored by God.

Can one be blessed while practicing things God condemns, things of the flesh, things like: fornication, uncleanness, loose conduct, idolatry, practice of spiritism, enmities, strife, jealousy, fits of anger, contentions, divisions, sects, envies, drunken bouts, revelries, and things like these.

Anyone who says he's blessed and yet practices any of the aforementioned things is not blessed, but is in fact cursed.

Chapter 12 HAIKU: BRIEF AND TO THE POINT

The following poems are written in the "Haiku" style. Haiku is a Japanese lyric poem of a fixed 17-syllable form. Haiku has only three lines, with five, seven, and five syllables. The rules for writing this brief poem are strict. Almost always some word must be used which refers to a season of the year. It is acceptable if the poem points to things or a pairing of things in nature that has moved the poet. I bent the rules only slightly to come up with my ten Haiku poems.

Haiku #1 Summer

Not as hot as hell,
the Bible hell is not hot
but it is summer.

Haiku #2 Fall

Breathtaking colors,
leaves fluttering as they sail
from the trees, it's fall.

Haiku #3 Winter

The weather outside
is frightful but its supposed
to be, it's winter.

Haiku #4 Spring

Behold the meadow
joyous birth is everywhere,
the reason, it's spring.

Haiku #5 The Rainbow

It's amazing that
many don't know the reason
why there's the rainbow.

Haiku #6 Why the Rainbow

The rainbow is a
sign from God, never again
a flood like Noah's.

Haiku #7 Day or Night

Some folks are good at
night, night people. What I
say is, give me the day.

Haiku #8 A Blanket

Have you ever seen
a blanket being made, not
of wool but of snow?

Haiku #9 What Time Is It?

Saw two big horned sheep
butting their heads like crazy
must be mating time.

Haiku #10 The Black Widow Male

They're hard luck spiders
the female bites his head off
right after they mate.

GOD IS GOOD

Attribute greatness to God
Bow down in worship to Him
Come before him with thanksgiving and praise
Declare among the nations his glory
Exult and be joyful in what God is doing
Fear inspiring and great is Jehovah
God of gods and Lord of lords is He
Happy is the people whose God is Jehovah
Inquire and they will tell you that
Jehovah is our Judge, King and Statute-giver
King of eternity He is, the only True God
Lean on Him and He will sustain you
Make melody to Him, tell others of His deeds
Never forsake Him and He will never forsake you
Obey his laws and commandments
Partake only of the table of Jehovah
Quench your thirst for knowledge from His Word
Read it in an undertone both day and night
Search for Jehovah while He may be found
Tell Him you want to serve Him and Him alone
Unburden all of your cares and worries upon Him
Voice to Him the desires of your heart
Willingly accept his counsel and discipline
'Xert yourself vigorously to gain his approval
Yoke yourself to his Son
Zealously serve Jehovah for He is good

ABOUT THE AUTHOR

Luther Whitley hails from Washington, D.C. and was educated in the D.C. Public School system. A building construction major, he is skilled in the major building trades including carpentry, electricity and plumbing and spends his time-off and vacations doing home remodeling. Whitley served four years in the U.S. Air Fore after finishing school and is currently employed with the United States Postal Service where he recently received an award and pin for thirty years of government service.

A voracious reader and serious student of the Scriptures, he spent many years in his church ministries, especially in speaking and teaching. Writing Bible discourses, songs and poems as well as attending writing seminars helped him to develop his writing skills.

It was his eighth grade English teacher he says who excited his interest in poetry. There were two poems that he fell in love with and immediately committed to memory. *Thanatopsis* by William Cullen Bryant and *The Raven* by Edgar Allen Poe. It was not until 1963 while in the Air Force stationed overseas that he did any serious writing. His first poem written back home to his wife was an acrostic poem titled *Distant Lovers* (Pg. 44).

In 1977 Luther created **Generosity Bible Game**, a board game in which the object was to be the first to give away all of one's property and possessions. More recently, he has authored two other books: **The Truth About Capital Punishment and Thou Shall Not Kill** and **Christmas: The Lie The Everybody Loves**.